Home Is Where the Heart Is

Thomas Kinkade

HARVEST HOUSE PUBLISHERS
EUGENE, OREGON 97402

Home Is Where the Heart Is

Where we love is home,

Home that our

feet may leave,

but not our hearts.

OLIVER WENDELL HOLMES

Home is a comfort
And home is a light
A place to leave the darkness outside
Home is a peaceful and ever-full feeling
A place where a soul safely hides
And being at home should remind you that still
There's a place that's prepared just for you
And I think my home is just heaven's reflection
As long as my home's here with you

Home is where someone is waiting and loving
And happy to see you again
That half of your heart
That somebody else treasures
The one who's your forever friend…

'Cause home is a comfort
And home is a light
A place to leave the darkness outside
Home is a peaceful and ever-full feeling
A place where a soul safely hides
And being at home should remind you that still
There's a place that's prepared just for you
And I think my home is just heaven's reflection
As long as my home's here with you

MICHAEL CARD

It was early evening when my journey began.

The train was full, but not yet uncomfortably full, of people going home....

The clicking of all those garden gates, the opening of all those front doors,

the unanalysable home smell in all those little halls,

the hanging up of all those hats, came over my imagination

with all the caress of a half-remembered bit of music.

There is an extraordinary charm in other people's domesticities.

Every lighted house, seen from the road, is magical:

every pram or lawn-mower in someone else's garden:

all smells or stirs of cookery from the windows of alien kitchens.

C. S. LEWIS
Present Concerns

As much as I converse

with sages and heroes,

they have very little of

my love and admiration.

I long for rural and

domestic scenes, for the

warbling of birds and the

prattling of my children.

JOHN ADAMS
Letter to his wife, March 16, 1777

I had three chairs in my house:

one for solitude, two for friendship, three for society.

HENRY DAVID THOREAU
Walden

Thomas Kinkade

A close-knit

and loving home

is worth more

than a kingdom.

WILLIAM BENNETT

It was the policy of the good old gentleman

to make his children feel that home

was the happiest place in the world;

and I value this delicious home-feeling

as one of the choicest gifts a parent can bestow.

WASHINGTON IRVING

Our natural and happiest life

is when we lose ourselves

in the exquisite

absorption of home...

MRS. MULOCK

Home, in one form or another,

is the great object of life.

JOSIAH G. HOLLAND

Stay, stay at home, my heart, and rest;

Home-keeping hearts are happiest,

For those that wander they know not where

Are full of trouble and full of care;

To stay at home is best.

HENRY WADSWORTH LONGFELLOW
Song

By wisdom a house is built,

and through understanding it is established;

through knowledge its rooms are filled

with rare and beautiful treasures.

THE BOOK OF PROVERBS

Sweet is the hour that brings us home,

Where all will spring to meet us;

Where hands are striving as we come,

To be the first to greet us.

When the world hath spent its frowns and wrath,

And care been sorely pressing;

'Tis sweet to turn from our roving path,

And find a fireside blessing.

Oh! Joyfully dear is the homeward track,

If we are but sure of a welcome back.

ELIZA COOK

Wherever smoke wreaths Heavenward curl—

Cave of a hermit, Hovel of churl,

Mansion of merchant, princely dome—

Out of the dreariness

Into its cheeriness,

Come we in weariness

Home.

STEPHEN CHALMERS
Home

No place is home until two people have latch keys.

ANONYMOUS

Every house where Love abides

And Friendship is a guest,

Is surely home, and home, sweet home;

For there the heart can rest.

HENRY VAN DYKE
Home Song

O fortunate, O happy day,

When a new household finds its place

Among the myriad homes of earth,

Like a new star just sprung birth.

DYER

'Mid pleasures and palaces

though we may roam,

Be it ever so humble,

there's no place like home.

JOHN HOWARD PAYNE

She lay back and listened to the little domestic sounds of the old house.

The fire whispered, a log shifted at its heart, the dog snored gently after his meal.

Outside, the wind stirred the trees, and somewhere a distant door banged as the breeze caught it.

Gradually, the peace that surrounded her took effect.

It had been a long day, and tomorrow would be an even harder one.

But meanwhile, the children slept as soundly as the dog on the rug at her feet,

and the night enfolded the quiet house.

MISS READ
No Holly for Miss Quinn

I see from my house by the side of the road,

By the side of the highway of life,

The men who press with the ardor of hope,

The men who are faint with the strife.

But I turn not away from their smiles nor their tears—

Both parts of an infinite plan;

Let me live in my house by the side of the road

And be a friend to man.

SAM WALTER FOSS

Every day they continued to meet together....

They broke bread in their homes and

ate together with glad and sincere hearts.

THE BOOK OF ACTS

The first glimpse of her new home was a delight to the eye and spirit....

The door of the little house opened,

and a warm glow of firelight flickered into the dusk.

Gilbert lifted Anne from the buggy and led her into the garden,

through the little gate between the ruddy-tipped firs,

up the trim, red path to the sandstone step.

"Welcome home," he whispered,

and hand in hand they

stepped over the threshold

of their house of dreams.

LUCY MAUD MONTGOMERY
Anne's House of Dreams

Home is where there is one to love us

Home's not merely four square walls,

Though with pictures hung and gilded;

Home is where affection calls—

Filled with shrines the hearth had builded!

Home! Go watch the faithful dove,

Sailing 'neath the heaven above us.

Home is where there's one to love us.

Home's not merely roof and room,

It needs something to endear it;

Home is where the heart can bloom,

Where there's some kind lip to cheer it!

What is home with none to meet,

None to welcome, none to greet us?

Home is sweet and only sweet,

Where there's one we love to meet us!

CHARLES SWAIN

"Ah! There is nothing like staying home for real comfort."

JANE AUSTEN
Emma

'Tis a little old house with a squeak in the stairs,

And a porch that seems made for just two easy chairs;

In the yard is a group of geraniums red,

And a glorious old-fashioned peony bed.

Petunias and pansies and larkspurs are there

Proclaiming their love for the old-fashioned pair.

Oh, it's hard now to picture the peace of the place!

Never lovelier smile lit a fair woman's face

Than the smile of the little old lady who sits

On the porch through the bright days of summer and knits.

And a courtlier manner no prince ever had

Than the little old man that she speaks of as "dad."

In that little old house there is nothing of hate;

There are old-fashioned things by an old-fashioned grate;

On the walls there are pictures of fine-looking men

And beautiful ladies to look at, and then

Time has placed on the mantel to comfort them there

The pictures of grandchildren, radiantly fair.

Every part of the house seems to whisper of joy,

Save the trinkets that speak of a lost little boy.

Yet Time has long since soothed the hurt and the pain,

And his glorious memories only remain:

The laughter of children the old walls have known,

And the joy of it stays, though the babies have flown.

I am fond of that house and that old-fashioned pair

And the glorious calm that is hovering there.

The riches of life are not silver and gold

But fine sons and daughters when we are grown old,

And I pray when the years shall have silvered our hair

We shall know the delights of that old-fashioned pair.

EDGAR A. GUEST

Blest be that spot,

where cheerful guests retire

To pause from toil, and time their evening fire!

Blest that abode,

where want and pain repair,

And every stranger finds a ready chair!

OLIVER GOLDSMITH

Cheerfully share your home

with those who need a meal

or a place to stay for the night.

THE BOOK OF 1 PETER

Sittin' on the porch at night when all the tasks are done,

Just restin' there an' talkin', with my easy slippers on,

An' my shirt band thrown wide open an' my feet upon the rail,

Oh, it's then I'm at my richest, with a wealth that cannot fail;

For the scent of early roses seems to flood the evening air,

An' a throne of downright gladness is my wicker rocking chair.

The dog asleep beside me, an' the children rompin' 'round

With their shrieks of merry laughter, Oh there is no gladder sound

To the ears o' weary mortals, spite of all the scoffers say,

Or a grander bit of music than the children at their play!

An' I tell myself times over, when I'm sittin' there at night,

That the world in which I'm livin' is a place o' real delight.

Then the moon begins its climbin' an' the stars shine overhead,

An' the mother calls the children an' she takes 'em up to bed,

An' I smoke my pipe in silence an' I think o' many things,

An' balance up my riches with the lonesomeness o' kings,

An' I come to this conclusion, an' I'll wager that I'm right—

That I'm happier than they are, sittin' on my porch at night.

EDGAR A. GUEST

An exile from home, splendor dazzles in vain;

Oh, give me my lowly thatched cottage again!

The birds singing gayly, that came at my call—

Give me them—and the peace of mind, dearer than all!

Home, home, sweet, sweet home!

There's no place like home, oh, there's no place like home!

JOHN HOWARD PAYNE
Home, Sweet Home

The little smiling cottage! Where at eve

He meets his rosy children at the door,

Prattling their welcomes, and his honest wife,

With good brown cake and bacon slice, intent

To cheer his hunger after the labor hard.

DYER

Home is where the heart is,

The soul's bright guiding star.

Home is where real love is,

Where our own dear ones are.

Home means someone waiting

To give a welcome smile.

Home means peace and joy and rest

And everything worthwhile.

AUTHOR UNKNOWN

Sweet are the joys of home,
And pure as sweet; for they,
Like dews of morn and evening, come
To wake and close the day.

The world hath its delights,
And its delusions, too;
But home to calmer bliss invites,
More tranquil and more true.

The mountain flood is strong,
But fearful in its pride;
While gently rolls the stream along
The peaceful valley's side.

Life's charities, like light,
Spread smilingly afar;
But stars approached, become more bright
And home is life's own star.

The pilgrim's step in vain
Seeks Eden's sacred ground!
But in home's holy joys, again
An Eden may be found.

JOHN BOWRING

my house

Lord, this humble house we'd keep

Sweet with play and calm with sleep.

Help us so that we may give

Beauty to the lives we live.

Let Thy love and let Thy grace

Shine upon our dwelling place.

EDGAR A. GUEST

Paintings